THEMES OF SONG:

A POEM,

READ BEFORE THE

AMPHICTYON ASSOCIATION,

OF THE

GENESEE WESLEYAN SEMINARY,

AT THE

ANNUAL EXHIBITION OF THAT INSTITUTION,

September 30th, 1842.

BY W. H. C. HOSMER.

Published by the Association.

ROCHESTER:

PRINTED BY WILLIAM ALLING, 12 EXCHANGE-STREET.

1842.

THEMES OF SONG.

I.

Where lives the soul of Poetry? It dwells
In the lone desert, where no fountain wells;
Speaks in the Kamsin's blast, dread foe of man,
That overthrows the luckless caravan;
And in a tomb, unknown to friendship, hides
The toiling camels and their Arab guides;
Dwells in the boiling mælstrom, deep and dark,
That roars a dismal warning to the bark,
And lingers where volcanic mountains throw
A burning deluge on the vale below.

II.

Where lives the soul of Poetry? Dark caves,
Worn by the foamy buffeting of waves;
The blue abysses of the moaning sea,
Where coral insects fashion dome and tree,

And mermaids chant, by mortal eye unseen,
And comb in sparry halls their tresses green;
The broad savannah, where the bison strays,
And come in herds the fallow-deer to graze;
The mossy forest, far from haunts of men,
Where the wild wolf prepares his savage den;
The giant Andes, round whose frosty peaks
The tempest hovers and the condor shrieks;
Cold, cheerless Greenland, where the ice-berg hoar
Strikes with a deafening crash the barren shore,
While roves the white fox and the polar bear,
In quest of prey, forsakes his icy lair;
Bright tropic bowers, within whose depths of green
The pard and savage tiger lurk unseen;
Where the fierce scales of deadly reptiles shine,
While round the trunks of giant palms they twine;
The spicy groves of Araby, the blest,
In fadeless robes of bloom and verdure drest;
Where birds of gorgeous plumage perch and sing
In varied strains, or wander on the wing;
Romantic Persia, where the dulcet lay
Of the glad Peri never dies away;
While the light pinions of the wooing wind
Fan the young leaves of date and tamarind,
And nightingales, amid the branches throng,
Own the glad presence of the *soul of song.*

III.

The rich, warm hues, that flush the western cloud
When yellow twilight weaves her glorious shroud;
The babbling cascade, that descends in foam
And flashing beauty from its rocky home;
The mingling tones of laughing earth and air,
When morn braids purple in her golden hair;
The dance of leaves, the lulling fall of rain,
The river, on its journey to the main;
The quiet lakes, that spread their sheets of blue,
A sweet enchantment lending to the view;
The fierce tornado, parent of dismay,
Uprooting sylvan giants in his way;
The lulling winds of summer, or the blast
That howls a requiem when the leaf is cast;
The pearly moon-shine of an autumn night,
When glen and glade are bathed in spectral light;
And lawn of spring, with varied flowers inwrought,
Are the pure nurses of poetic thought.

IV.

Go where Parnassus lifts his hoary brow,
Though classic Delphi lies in ruin now,
And the grim robber lurks, with wary eye,
Round the rich fount of storied Castaly;
Stroll where the walks of Tempe, broad and green,

Proud Ossa and Olympus spread between,
While through bright bowers the swift Peneus strays,
And foamy tribute to Ægean pays.
The bearded corsair, chants in foreign tongue,
Where the blind king of epic grandeur sung;
No voice of onset rises from the plain,
Where rapt Tyrteus woke the martial strain;
Thine isle, oh, Sappho! mourning waters gird,
But there no music like thine own is heard;
Where the proud mother, hurried to the field
Her only son, and giving him a shield,
Said, with an accent of heroic joy,
"*Bring, or be brought upon it back, my boy*"*!*
Now Grecian girls their tinkling rebecks string,
And the soft magic of the Blind God sing—
By moon-light gaily link their rosy hands,
And dance the glad Romaika on the sands.
In beauty still the tumbling billows break
On the lone shore of Lerna's reedy lake,
Still the green olive trembles in the breeze,
Though there no Hydra roves—no Hercules;
Pactolus glides, to deathless beauty wed,
But gold no longer flashes in his bed—
Above that sea the sky still looks divine,
Where Delos darted from the cradling brine—
The tide yet sweeps where blushing Venus rose,
But Triton there his horn no longer blows.

V.

Go where the top of old Hymettus towers—
Haunt of the bee, and odorous with flowers,
While far below, the cool Cephissus winds;
A name of kindling fire to classic minds,
Pause, where the streams of wooded Ida flow;
Though guardian Naiads fled, long, long ago:
The verdant sides of dewy Latmos climb,
Rich in the precious lore of olden time;
Where star-girt Dian, from her throne of blue,
Came down the young Endymion to woo—
Stand on old hills that overlook the seas,
Though gone their nymphs, the wild Oreades—
In fancy view the dolphin cleave the wave,
And bear the minstrel from a watery grave;
Hear proud Amphion wake his master-tone,
And give life, joy, mobility to stone;
On old Egina fix your kindling glance—
Round Athens linger in poetic trance—
The sacred groves of fallen Greece explore;
Home of the laughing Dryades no more,
And own, although her star of power hath set,
The soul of kingly Song is present yet.

VI.

The sun looks fondly on the crumbling dome,
And fallen pile of desecrated Rome,
And the wan moon her horn of silver fills,
To bathe in dazzling light her seven hills—
As rolled his wave when Italy was free,
Still rolls old father Tiber to the sea:
Morn, on his breast a red enchantment throws,
His waves still blush when day is near its close,
And floating sweetly through majestic trees,
Come the wild songs of herdsmen on the breeze.
Though creeping ivy veils imperial wrecks,
And the dark brow of victor ruin decks—
Though nodding weeds of loneliness are high
Where marble triumphs of the chisel lie—
Though the dark bat and solitary toad,
Find in the hall of Cæsar an abode;
No longer hung with hostile banners furled,
And trophies wrested from a subject world—
Though wall-flowers grow beside the prostrate shrine,
And mingling piles that cumber Palatine,
A voice of many tones goes up from wave,
Dark ruin, storied haunt, and green old grave.
It whispers of past triumphs, when the street
Was strewn with flowery carpets for the feet;
When wreathy clouds of grateful incense rose

From smoking altars, white as drifted snows:
When horse and foot went by with iron clang;
While the shrill trump and brazen clarion rang—
When came the captive host and spoils of war
Behind the victor in his glittering car,
With golden ball, refulgent on his breast,
In flowing robes of kingly purple drest.

VII.

A voice goes up from Numa's sacred mount,
Deserted temple and neglected fount,
From snowy columns piled in fluted heaps,
And the round tomb, where proud Metella sleeps;
From emptied urn, and broken arch of stone
That breathes a saddening tale of glory gone:
That voice, like echo in sepulchral halls,
On the quick ear of musing genius falls,
His spirit pluming for a flight sublime,
While round him rise the wasting wrecks of time.
Where Brutus bared the steel, Childe Harold heard
That voice of mourning, and his soul was stirred,
Swept his proud harp beneath Ausonian skies,
And woke his wildest, sweetest melodies.
When music trembled on the evening breeze,
And moon-beams lighted architrave and frieze
Within the lofty Coliseum stood,

The Lord of Newstead, in his saddest mood,
On the square block and corridor beheld
The mark of Vandal, and the stain of eld,
While the pale light through broken arches stole,
To deck decay, and beautify the whole.
The Pilgrim thought of men ignobly brave,
The purpled master, and submissive slave,
Whose voices wildly mingled in one yell
Of savage pleasure when some victim fell.
Fresh grew his memory of those golden days,
When Flaccus chanted his immortal lays—
Gave point and polish to satiric shaft,
While glad Apollo praised his skill and laughed;
When tuneful Maro, epic monarch, strung
His lyre of deathless harmony and sung:
The daring pinion of his fancy spread,
And fadeless lustre on old Ilium shed:
When graceful Tully in the forum spoke,
Enkindled anger, or amazement woke,
While the fell traitor, pale with terror, heard
The knell of crime in each denouncing word.
Back on his mind came that terrific night
When dreaming thousands woke in wild affright;
When the loud blast of Gothic trumpets fell
On Roman ears of hope the horrid knell,
And through rent gates, with lance and lifted sword,

Came Alaric, the mighty, and his horde.
Oh, dreadful hour! when startled Tiber ran
Red with the light of flames and blood of man,
When blazing domes changed darkness into day;
Enticing Lust to Innocence, his prey.
Where was thy matchless race of iron men,
Thy victor eagle, queen of empires, then?
What strange mutation in thy heart was wrought?
Thy children *trembled* where their fathers *fought*—
Thy Bird of Conquest, like a timid thing,
With drooping neck and darkly folded wing,
Saw kneeling matrons, red with infant gore,
In vain the wild barbarian implore.

VIII.

Though Rome is fallen from her high estate,
Her grandeur gone, her palace desolate;
Although her haughty flag no longer flings
On trampled lands the shadow of its wings,
She is the home of memories that stir
With inspiration all who visit her;
The wondrous magnet of thy world, oh, Thought!
By wisdom haunted, and by scholar sought—
Where the proud sons of Taste and Science find
Forever spread the festival of mind.
The sybyl of Egeria hath fled—

Where Cato trod assassins boldly tread—
Across hėr bridge that spans the troubled tide
Pomp moves no longer with collossal stride—
Gone are the genii of her bowers and plains,
But the sweet soul of deathless Song remains.

IX.

Land of the Holy Sepulchre! thou art
The noblest theme to rouse poetic heart,
For every rock beneath thy glowing sky
Hath rung with kindling tones of prophecy:
On the bright mountains of thy clime have trod
The sweet, seraphic Messengers of God—
With the pure presence of that Lamb who died
To save a world thy rivers are allied:
Within thy bowers, and groves of beauty rare,
His meek diciples have knelt down in prayer;
The dying martyr, in exulting strains
Hath sung of triumph on thy sacred plains,
And saints have often meekly bent the knee
On the green shore of breezy Galilee.

X.

Through wasted vales, in rich barbaric garb,
The haughty emir guides his flying barb;
Above the sod of apostolic graves

The pallid glory of the cresent waves—
Where the swift Arnon in his channel foams
The dusky reader of the Koran roams;
Where Carmel rises, rich in sacred lore,
Goes up the smoke of sacrifice no more—
The sons of Islam pitch their tents of snow
Where rang the harp and tymbrel long ago;
Where the winged angel woke the dreaming wave,
And healing power to cool Bethesda gave.
The cry of "*Allah!*" on each wind that blows
Is borne where Sharon gloried in her rose,
Where Hermon shone, with heavenly dew-drops wet,
And Beauty made her home on Olivet.
Though on the banks of Jordan now are mute
The notes of sackbut, dulcimer and lute,
Still the proud cedar lifts his verdant cone,
And makes the top of Lebanon his throne.
Bright robes of glory still inyest the place,
Where dwelt the parents of the human race,
Still Horeb towers whereon the Prophet stood
When the mad whirlwind shook the crashing wood,
Heard the loud thunder in the vaulted sky,
And knew Jehovah by his flashing eye.
Oh, words are feeble vehicles of thought
To paint a clime where miracles were wrought,
Unless the tongue that gives them voice can sing
Like rapt Isaiah or the Shepherd King.

XI.

Go where the Nile, to slake the torrid sand,
Leaps from his bed, and overflows the land—
Where the red sun-burst of the morning hour
The harp of Memnon woke with mystic power—
Where lofty Science from her cradle sprung,
And over Greece her burning mantle flung;
Where infant sculpture made the marble warm,
To wondrous sphinx and hippogrif gave form,—
Where Memphis boasted of her wealth untold,
Her spacious halls of porphyry and gold:
Where the proud Queen of Victors* brightly wove
Round Roman hearts the matchless spell of love,
Lifted the gilded beaker to her lip,
In one proud draught the wealth of kings to sip—
Lay on her blazing couch of queenly rest,
By Cupids fanned, voluptuously drest,
While her swift galley down the Cydnus flew
Rich in its freight, and sail of purple hue,
Spread out by winds that bore the tone of lute,
And the low warblings of the dulcet flute.
O, mourning Mother of lost arts! thy name
Stirs with unwonted sympathy my frame—
Wakes in my heart affection's holiest thrill,
Although thy ruins whiten vale and hill.

* Cleopatra.

I know that Turkish conquest in a day
Thy heaps of letter'd wisdom swept away,
That turbaned pachas wield the scourging rod
Where Ptolemy and proud Sesostris trod,
But still thy fount of lore by Learning sought,
Gives sight to Blindness, and a glow to Thought.

XII.

In fancy visit that neglected site
Where Carthage rose in majesty and might,
By Dido founded on old Afric's strand,
With Neptune subject to her dread command.
That Chief recall who left his ocean-home
To battle for the mastery with Rome—
Across the frosty Alps his legions led,
While kingdoms shook beneath his iron tread—
Recall her peerless ships of old renown
That long ago beneath the wave went down—
Think of her awful destiny, and pour
A wail for grandeur that will live no more ;
No vestige lingers of her triple walls,
Her flanking towers, her storm-proof arsenals ;
Of her strong bulwarks sword, and fire, and time,
To charm the gaze, have left no wreck sublime,
The laurel crown is faded on her brow—
Amid her ruins sits no Marius now ;

For Empire lost, and Glory in the grave
There is no mourner, save the chainless wave.

XIII.

Ye solemn Cities of the Dead !—bereft
Of brightness, being ; ye have something left—
A power to wake the pulses of the soul,
And back the darkling tide of ages roll—
A charm that robs pale Silence of his chain,
And fills with light the chambers of the brain ;
A talismanic witchery that calls
The shrouded mighty from their charnel halls,
Fills air with regal spectres, while the hand
Of buried Magic grasps a broken wand—
Calls the fierce chieftain from forgotten tomb,
With breast-plate, greave, strong helm and nodding plume,
To wake with trump wan multitudes of slain,
And lead them madly to the field again.
Ye Haunts of lofty musing ! though the flood
Of wild invasion merged your pomp in blood,
Though column huge and obelisk of taste
Lie darkly buried in the sandy waste,
Though the tall ostrich flaps his stately wings,
And bitterns boom above the dust of kings—
Though in your courts the ministers of death
Breathe on the wind their pesilential breath,

Ye have a mystic potency of spell
That sways the bosom to its inmost cell,
A magic lamp that sheds redeeming day
On desolation, darkness, and decay.

XIV.

Romantic Spain, for years of glory flown,
Breathes on the wind her melancholy moan ;
No more the pennon of her Cid will wave
Its green, triumphant folds above the brave,
But roving Fancy, in her olive bowers,
To charm mankind still culls poetic flowers—
Finds tale of wonder on her lonely strand,
And warlike legend in her mountain-land—
Strolls where Grenada lifts her verdant hill
On which the tall Alhambra glitters still
Rich in its fret-work, and Mosaic floor,
That echoes back the tread of kings no more.
On the fair banks of gentle Rio Verde,
In dreams again the Moorish horn is heard,
While Leon, waking with a battle shout,
Lifts the red lance, and flings her banner out.

XV.

Land of the Claymore, and the rugged rock,
Burn, broomy knowe, gray cairn, and stormy loch

On the proud altar of thy bardic fame
Full brightly burns imperishable flame!
With partial art Apollo tuned thy lyre,
And tone celestial gave each trembling wire—
No brighter stars within his temple shine,
Land of the pibroch and the plaid, than thine!
No more thy Fingal, when the camp is still,
Moves in his armor on the windy hill,
With ghostly Trenmor dialogue to hold,
While awfully roll back the times of old.
No more the sons of woody Morven throng
With shield and helmet to the hall of song,
Call on the bard to weave his mystic spells,
And lend enchantment to the feast of shells;
Borne on the pinions of the hollow blast.
No more dark Loda's spirit journeys past,
But Ossian lives, and in his bardic crown
Gleams the rich germ of thy mature renown.

XVI.

Thy heart within its greenest cell inurns
The lasting, lofty memory of Burns,
And proudly throbs when seek the pilgrim throng
His lowly cot and scenery of his song—
Stand on the banks of wooded Ayr, or tune
Their harps to praise him in the bowers of Doon.

Thy sad, decaying fabrics of the past,
Gloom on the relics of the mighty cast—
Fair Melrose Abbey holds in solemn trust
The heart of Bruce and Douglass, changed to dust;
The roof of Dryburg bends above the place
Where rest lost scions of a noble race,
And the fresh grave where Scott lies darkly shrined,
The crowning rose in thy proud wreath of mind.
Tweed, Carron, Nith, Sweet Clyde, romantic Dee,
And all thy streams that journey to the sea—
Ben Nevis, Lomond, Cruachan, Cairn, Gorm,
And all thy peaks that battle with the storm—
Thy yawning caves, green shaws, romantic dells,
Where brownies gather, and the warlock dwells,
And lonely moors, with heather overspread,
His muse to immortality hath wed.

XVII.

Land of the Shamrock—Island of the brave!
Thy broad, green fields are trodden by the slave;
But my weak hand one flower of song will cast
On the dark tomb that hides thy buried Past.
Dim is thy 'scutcheon with obscuring dust,
And dark thy spear with thick corroding rust;
The Sword of Breffni, with its terror gone,
Hangs in its scabbard blunted and undrawn;

No garland braids thy brow of settled gloom—
Thy red-haired chieftain hath a noteless tomb—
No banner floats from Tara's mouldered walls,
And heard no more is harping in thy halls.
Gone is the *Child* who wept thy waning day,
Woke on thy mournful shore Funereal lay,
Flowing so wildly sweet to mortal ear,
That even mailed Oppression paused to hear.
The gate of Grandeur and the cottage door
Are open flung to welcome him no more—
Thy lonely exile, under distant skies,
Starts at the name of Carolan and sighs,
True Bard, who perished warbling to life's close
Thy song of sorrow, and thy tale of woes!

XVIII.

Thy Curran, Grattan, Sheridan, and Flood,
In the bright van-guard of the mighty stood,
And roused, to rend thy unrelaxing chain,
The thunders of their eloquence in vain.
In bondage thus thou givest birth to sons
Whom Earth enrolls among her mighty ones;
What would thy children be if they awoke,
And every strand in Grief's black cable broke?
Lamps in the Hall of Freedom to the blind—
Gems of the world, bright polar stars of mind.

XIX.

Oh, Erin! yet a pulse beats in thy soul,
Thy hand hath dashed to earth the damning bowl—
One tear is wiped from off thy cheek of wo,
Pledge that thy star another morn will know,
While brave men wronged, march forth in stern array,
To roll from Glory's tomb the stone away.
Though bondage, block, invading host, and sword,
A gory deluge on thy head have poured,
The flower of genius, watered by thy tears,
Blooms 'mid the pleading wrecks of former years.
Swept by a Moore, the harp of Innisfail
Gives out complaining murmur to the gale:
He found the matchless instrument unstrung,
On its cold frame the spider's web-work hung;
Beneath his hand, from chords for ages hushed,
Rich streams of wild, delicious music gushed;
Oh, may the Minstrel, ere he looks his last
On thy green fields, revived, behold the past—
Thy "*Sun-Burst,*" glittering on the gale once more;
Thy long night ended, and thy heart-ache o'er.
Too long have sable vestments wrapped thy form—
Too long howled round thy naked head the storm,
In Freedom's Temple, rescued from disgrace,
The *Lear of nations* yet shall find a place.

XX.

The peerless Isle that gave our fathers birth,
Hath many spots of consecrated earth;
Though Victor Time, in his remorseless march,
Hath worn the cloister dim, and Gothic arch—
Left stain of darkness on the tomb of pride,
Where Strength and Beauty slumber side by side;
Trace back her story to that distant day,
When tuneful Merline woke the bardic lay,
And the wild Briton, in his savage car,
Met, with bare breast, the Roman shock of war.
No daring son of Cader Idris, now
Sleeps in the cavern, on his rocky brow,
While wizzards string his harp with glowing chords,
And give his tongue the gift of burning words;
But the rude pile of Stonehenge still uprears
Colossal fragments dark with cloudy years;
Each rugged rock of Druidism tells—
Shrines red with gore, and wild, unholy spells.
No more the priest, in robe of snowy fold,
Climbs the tall oak with knife of gleaming gold,
And cuts, while chant the mystic throng below,
Balm for all ill, the precious mistletoe.
No more the victim vainly shrieks for aid,
The groves of Mona in the dust are laid,

And the bright Star of Bethlehem sheds light
On the dense vapor of Druidic night.

XXI.

No more Old England hears, in good greenwood,
The merry bugle of her Robin Hood;
His bow is broken, and entombing mould
Roofs the dark mansion of his outlaws bold;
From her green glens, like misty shapes, have gone
The merry court of Monarch Oberon.
No more the gaze of wondering Romance
Beholds her fairy throng prolong the dance,
When mellow star-light gives a lustrous glow
To Cam and gentle Avon as they flow:
No more beholds her Knight throw down the glove,
And couch the lance to please his lady-love—
Tilt in the tourney against fearful odds,
While beauty waves her 'kerchief and applauds.
No more her Richard draws the fatal sword,
To smite the fiery Soldan and his horde,
But castled wrecks of feudal grandeur still
Crown, with their mossy battlements, her hill,
And airy Fable seeks old haunted springs
To gem with dew her *ever-changing* wings;
Her gray, monastic ruins, darkly keep
Their lonely vigils on her blooming steep;

Her princely homes, round which the ivy twines,
Tell olden tales of her Baronial lines,
When winking Mirth on Valor fondly gazed,
Then to his lip the cup of wassail raised—
Or murder bared his deadly knife, and found
Tomb for his prey in dungeons under ground.
On battle plain where now the heifer feeds,
The clang of armor, and the rush of steeds,
At midnight, startle the belated swain,
And chill the red warm current in his vein.

XXII.

Oh, Land of Inspiration! where the Nine
Came to uprear an everlasting shrine,
When blood was mingled with Castalian dew,
And dark with cloud the sky of Hellas grew—
Thy queenly name and Lion Flag are known
From the parched Tropic to the Frozen Zone.
What true descendant of the Pilgrim stock,
Who shouted "Freedom!" on the Plymouth Rock,
Feels not true pride, green jewel of the sea,
To think he drew his parentage from thee?
Well may the children of thy rock-bound coast,
Tell of thy fame to every land, and boast,
"Here Chaucer wrote, and Spencer swept the lyre,
With tuneful ear and necromantic fire;

Here nursing Nature, with caresses fond,
To Shakspeare gave her wonder-working wand;
Smiled, when her idol, with one mighty stroke,
A boundless sea of thought and feeling woke;
Here the bright muse of Milton, spurning earth,
With angels sang, where light and life have birth;
Then flying downward, by an awful spell,
Laid bare the dreadful mysteries of Hell!

XXIII.

Though storied Europe, of the past may boast,
Her heirs of deathless fame, a countless host!
Presiding spirits over mount and vale,
Dark haunt of ghost, and legendary tale—
Tombs of the mighty, and the wrecks of art,
That stir, with mournful memories, the heart;
Our own free land is rich in glorious themes,
And lofty sources of poetic dreams.
Earth, that conceals the dust of patriot sires,
No pompous aid from fading art requires;
Above their bones no pyramid uprears
Its grand proportions mystical with years;
The mounds that mark the places of their rest,
Poetic rapture kindle in the breast;
Instill a love of country that will brave
Despotic wrath on land or rolling wave.

Their blood, by which our liberty was bought,
Hath sanctified the places where they fought;
And when the Muse of History unseals
Her mighty tome, deep, thrilling joy she feels
When pointing out, amid the names that fill
With light her fadeless pages, "BUNKER HILL!"

XXIV.

We, too, have dark memorials of the past,
With cloudy robes of doubt around them cast!
And plodding Science, to dispel the shade,
In vain calls wild conjecture to her aid.
Our Western caves, within their wombs of stone,
Hide mortal wrecks, to memory unknown;
Bones of the mammoth, that appall the gaze,
Majestic relics of departed days!
And broad, green prairies, in their sweep infold
Vast mounds constructed by the tribes of old.

XXV.

Where can the children of Apollo find
More lovely haunts to please romantic mind
Than those that grace our own green land of woods,
Fair skies, bright vales, and fertilizing floods?
Clad in the gaudy costume of his race,
Here the fleet red man panted in the chase,

Swept the light paddle, or in thickest shade
For painted foe the deadly ambush laid.
Here the broad boughs of sylvan giants wove
His green cathedral in the mossy grove—
Beneath its roof, an altar-stone he raised,
And the Great Spirit of his people praised,
Read his kind mercy in the sun-light warm,
His anger in the whirl-wind and the storm.
Like some proud oak when lightning scathes the rind,
That lives awhile, then falls before the wind,
While fragrant flowers of evanescent dyes,
That loved its shadows, droop and close their eyes—
So when the whites applied the *worm of grief*
To the dark bosom of the Indian chief,
He fell a ruin, and his tribe in vain
Mourn for the limits of their old domain,
And broken-hearted, follow, one by one,
His path to isles below the setting sun.

XXVI.

Our mossy groves and mighty inland seas,
That bare their broad, blue bosoms to the breeze;
Our lofty hills, that guard the fruitful vale
Rich in tall forests bending to the gale;
Our mighty stretch of coast, from sea to sea,
Where man alone to God inclines the knee;

Where, free from gale, with canvass idly furled,
Might snugly moor the shipping of the world;
Our streams, embracing in ther winding arms,
All that enchanted vision chains or charms;
And Niagara, when the storm is loud,
Who drowns the deep roar of the thunder-cloud,
Clad in his bright, magnificent array,
Of rain-bow, storm, white foam, and torrent spray,
Woo genius forth to win a crown of light,
And plume his pinion for an Epic flight—
From air invoke Divinities to guard
Glen, grot, and mountain, sacred to the Bard.

XXVII.

The hand of Fame no purer wreath can twine
Round mortal brow, sweet Poesy, than thine!
For blushing carnage and the tear of grief
Dim not the beauty of its fadeless leaf—
And the fresh odors of its bloom impart
Balm to the bitter ailments of the heart.
Who, who would fling thy precious flowers away,
To gird his temples with heroic bay,
Or tread in dust thy garland of renown
To snatch from pomp his regal robe and crown?
Oh, not true Bard and holy in whose breast
The wave of earthly passion is at rest!

XXVIII.

When gentle Music, sister Art, is mute—
Her viol broken, and unstrung her lute,
When the proud triumphs of the painter fade,
Lose their rich tinting, and grow dark with shade—
While sculpture mourns her form of breathing stone,
By cruel change and Vandal overthrown,
While Taste beholds her fairest fabrics fall,
And o'er them Nature weave her ivied pall—
While charm the sons of Thespis for a day,
Then melt, like dew-drops of the night, away,
While Conquest moulders in his martial shroud,
A rayless star behind a dusky cloud—
While cities slumber in volcanic graves,
And isles of beauty sink beneath the waves,
The bright creations of the Poet live,
And joy to passing generations give—
Borne on the wandering winds of every clime
Assault defying of Decay and Time.

XXIX.

Where is the Land of Song? oh, not alone
To famous fields where War his trump hath blown,
And Earth's proud places are its bounds confined:
It owns a royal Empire in the mind:
Beyond the bright blue curtain of the skies,

Where living verdure fadeth not, it lies—
No clouds obscure the radiant prospect there,
And ever throbs with melody the air:
Oh, there, at last, a harp will minstrel wake
Whose silver chord no rending blast will break,
There, in full tide, will his free numbers flow,
There will his strain no *dying cadence know.*

N O T E S .

Note 1.—*With golden ball refulgent on his breast.*

Stanzas vi.

"The general (Dux) came drest in purple, embroidered with gold, (*toga picta et tunica palmata*) with a crown of laurel on his head, a branch of laurel in his right hand, and in his left an ivory sceptre, with an eagle on the top, having his face painted with vermillion, in like manner as the statue of Jupiter, on festival days, and a golden ball (*aurea bulla*) hanging from his neck on his breast, with some amulet in it, or magical preservative against envy.—*Adams' Roman Ant. p.* 327.

Note 2.—*Gone is the child who wept thy waning day,*
Woke on thy mournful shore funeral lay.

Stan. xvii.

"Carolan Twalogh, a celebrated poet and musical composer, justly styled the Irish Handel, was born in the year 1670, in the village of Nabber, in the county of Westmeath, on the lands of Carolan's town, which formerly belonged to his ancestors. The cabin, in which the bard was born, is still pointed out to the inquiring traveller. It is now in a ruinous state, and must soon become a prey to all-devouring time; yet the spot where it stood, will perhaps be visited at a future day, by the lovers of national music and song, with as much true devotion as the birth-place of Shakspeare, or the cottage of Burns. The small-pox deprived him of sight at so early a period, that he retained no recollection of colors; yet, from this misfortune, he felt no uneasiness, and was never heard to complain. '*My eyes,*' he used to say, '*are transplanted to my ears.*' He married Mary M'Guire, a young lady of good family in the county of Fermanagh; and shortly after, fixed his residence on a small farm near Moss-hill, in the county of Leitrim. His ardent hospitality soon consumed the produce of his farm; he ate, drank, and was merry, and imprudently left to-morrow to provide for itself. This mode of life soon occasioned embarrassments in his domestic affairs, and he resolved to become an itinerant harper and bard, in which character he continued during the remainder of his life; travelling through the country, mounted on a good horse, attended by a domestic on another, who carried his harp. Wherever he went, the gates of the nobility and gentry were thrown open to him; he was received with respect, and a distinguished place assigned him at table. Carolan, while on a visit to Mrs. M'Dermott's, of Alderford, in the county of Rosscommon, was taken suddenly ill, and died there, in the month of March, 1738, in the 68th year of his age; and was interred in the parish church of Kilrouan, in the diocese of Ardagh. But no memorial exists of the spot in which his remains were laid."—*Bunting's Music of Ireland.*

NOTE 3.—*Thy "sun-burst" glittering on the gale once more.*

STAN. XIX.

The "sun-burst," was the fanciful name given by the ancient Irish to the Royal Banner.

"For high was thy hope, when those glories were darting
Around thee, thro' all the gross clouds of the world;
When Truth from her fetters indignantly starting,
At once, like a Sun-burst her banner unfurled."—*Moore.*

NOTE 4.—*No daring son of Cader Idris now*
Sleeps in the cavern on his rocky brow.

STAN. XX.

On the summit of the Cader Idris, is a cave, made an object of interest to the tourist, by the songs of ancient Welch Bards. A belief still prevails among the peasantry, that the individual who passes the night within the cave, will descend the mountain either crazed, or inspired with the gift of song.

" From Snowden, a line of mountains extends to Phinlimmon, a boundary of North Wales; of these mountains, the most lofty, and the most celebrated, is Cader Idris. In height, it is the second in Wales. It rises on the sea shore, about a mile from Lorogn. Its ascent is gradual, first in a northerly direction, for about three miles; then for about ten miles east north-east. From its summit, a branch spreads out in a south-west direction, nearly three miles long, which is parallel to the main ridge. On all sides, it is steep and craggy; but the southern side is almost perpendicular. It is about three thousand five hundred and forty feet above the level of the sea, which is eighty yards higher than any of the mountains in Cumberland.—*Edinburgh Encyc. vol. viii. p.* 505.

NOTE 5.—*No more the priest, in robe of snowy fold,*
Climbs the tall oak with knife of gleaming gold.

STAN. XX.

" According to Pliny, the Druids held nothing so sacred as the mistletoe of the oak; they believed that every thing which grew upon that tree, came from Heaven. Whenever the mistletoe was discovered upon it, they went with great ceremony to gather it. The sixth day of the moon was always chosen for the purpose. In their own language, the Druids called the mistletoe, *all-healing*. As soon as they had prepared, under the oak, all the appliances for sacrifice, and the banquet which they usually made, they tied, for the first time, two white bulls to it by the horns. Then one of the priests, clothed in white, ascends the tree, and with a golden knife cuts off the mistletoe, which is received in a white garment. After this, sacrifices are offered up. The word *Druid*, is sometimes erroneously confounded with that of Bard. The one, composed hymns to gods; the other, celebrated the achievements of heroes. It appears that in Wales, there was an annual Congress of Bards usually held at the royal residence, the Sovereign himself, presiding. Here, each was assigned a preference and emolument suitable to his merit; but the Bard most highly distinguished for his talents, was solemnly chaired and honored with the badge of a silver chain. The Bards, properly so called, were distinguished from the Druids, and from the Eubates, (whose office it was to celebrate religious rites,) by the color of their dress—they were clad in *sky-blue garments*, while the Druids wore *white*, and

the Eubates, *green*. There were four principal meetings of the Bards held in the course of the year, viz: at the two solstices, and the two equinoxes. The first, was at the winter solstice, which was the beginning of the year, and called *Alvan Arthan*. The second, at the vernal equinox, called *Alvan Eiler*—the summer solstice, or *Alvan Hevin*—and autumnal equinox, or *Alvan Elved*, follows next in order.

"They assembled in circles of unwrought stones, placed so as to be indexes of the seasons—in the open air, and always where the sun was above the horizon: or, as they expressed it, '*in the face of the sun, and in the eye of the light.*'"—*Warton's His. of English Poetry—Jones' Relics of Welsh Bards.*

NOTE 6.—*Our Western Caves, within their wombs of stone,*
Hide mortal wrecks to memory unknown.

STAN. XXIV.

In the Caves of Kentucky, mummies have been found in a state of wonderful preservation, though unprotected by coffin or shroud, from the wasting effects of a humid atmosphere. The Indian tribes, through the medium of tradition, can give no conjecture, even as to their history. Implements found with them, however, indicate considerable progress in civilization and the arts.

www.ingramcontent.com/pod-product-compliance
Lightning Source LLC
LaVergne TN
LVHW010743120826
845150LV00009B/2279

* 9 7 8 1 4 1 8 1 9 4 7 5 8 *